The Bald Eagle

by Norman Pearl

illustrated by Matthew Skeens

PICTURE WINDOW BOOKS
Minneapolis, Minnesota

Special thanks to our advisers for their expertise:

Melodie Andrews
Associate Professor of Early American and Women's History
Minnesota State University, Mankato

Susan Kesselring, M.A., Literacy Educator
Rosemount–Apple Valley–Eagan (Minnesota) School District

Editor: Nick Healy
Designer: Abbey Fitzgerald
Page Production: Melissa Kes
Art Director: Nathan Gassman
Associate Managing Editor: Christianne Jones
The illustrations in this book were created digitally.

Picture Window Books
5115 Excelsior Boulevard, Suite 232
Minneapolis, MN 55416
877-845-8392
www.picturewindowbooks.com

Printed in the United States of America.

Library of Congress Cataloging-in-Publication Data
Pearl, Norman.
The bald eagle / by Norman Pearl ; illustrated by Matthew Skeens.
p. cm. — (American symbols)
Includes bibliographical references and index.
ISBN-13: 978-1-4048-2642-7 (library binding)
ISBN-10: 1-4048-2642-4 (library binding)
ISBN-13: 978-1-4048-2645-8 (paperback)
ISBN-10: 1-4048-2645-9 (paperback)
1. United States—Seal—Juvenile literature. 2. Bald eagle—United States—Juvenile
literature. 3. Emblems, National—United States—Juvenile literature. 4. Animals—
Symbolic aspects—Juvenile literature. I. Skeens, Matthew. II. Title.
CD5610.P42 2007
929.9—dc22   2006027218

Table of Contents

Hi! I'm **Bill the bird keeper**. I work at a wildlife center. One of my favorite animals is the bald eagle. The bald eagle is very important to the people of the United States. Keep reading to learn more about this special bird.

The bald eagle is also known as the American eagle.

The National Emblem

The bald eagle is a large and powerful bird. It is a great flier and hunter. It is also the national emblem of the United States. The emblem is a symbol standing for the whole nation.

More than 200 years ago, the Founding Fathers picked the bald eagle as the national emblem. The Founding Fathers were a group of leaders who helped form the United States. They wanted a very special animal to represent their new and growing country.

Why the Bald Eagle?

The Founding Fathers wanted a symbol of strength, courage, and freedom. The bald eagle looked proud and strong in flight. It was beautiful, too.

The American leaders also wanted a symbol of loyalty. The bald eagle is a loyal bird. It usually has just one mate for life. A bald eagle will take another partner only if its first mate dies.

The bald eagle can be found as far north as Alaska and northern Canada. It has been spotted as far south as northern Mexico.

Lastly, the Founding Fathers wanted an animal found in the United States. Here, too, the bald eagle fit perfectly. It lives only in North America.

The Eagle and the Turkey

Not everyone liked the bald eagle. One famous Founding Father, Benjamin Franklin, preferred the wild turkey. Unlike barnyard turkeys, wild turkeys roam free. Flocks of wild turkeys live in North American forests. They feed on insects, fruits, and nuts.

Benjamin Franklin described the bald eagle as a bird of "bad moral character." He said that because bald eagles kill other animals for food and sometimes steal food from other animals.

A wild turkey is not as strong or as beautiful as a bald eagle. Still, Franklin described the wild turkey as "a much more respectable choice."

The Founding Fathers argued about the national emblem for more than six years. In the end, the bald eagle won out. It became our national emblem and our national bird.

Using the Emblem

Pictures of the bald eagle are all around. In the United States, the bald eagle is on silver dollars, half dollars, and quarters. Its picture has also appeared on many postage stamps.

The bald eagle is on the Great Seal of the United States, too. The Great Seal is a mark used by the government. It is put on important government documents. The Great Seal is also shown on the back of one-dollar bills.

On the Great Seal, the bald eagle has a scroll in its mouth. The Latin words *E Pluribus Unum* are on the scroll. They mean "out of many, one." These words describe the United States, which is one nation made up of many states.

Symbol of Freedom

Many early Americans knew a legend, or story, about the bald eagle. The story said that bald eagles circled over American soldiers in an early Revolutionary War battle. The birds shrieked loudly. Soldiers believed that the birds were crying out for freedom. Some people said the eagles gave soldiers the courage to keep fighting.

In the 1700s, bald eagles were fairly common in North America. But in time, the number of eagles shrank. The birds lost their forest homes as people built towns and cleared farm fields.

The bald eagle has no natural enemies in the wild. It is harmed only by humans.

A Special Animal

Bald eagles fly through the sky with speed and ease. The birds can weigh up to 14 pounds (6.3 kilograms). They are about 3 feet (0.9 meters) tall. That is about as tall as an average 3-year-old child. Bald eagles have white heads and tails and yellow eyes. Their bodies are covered with brown feathers.

Have you ever heard the term "eagle eyes"? It means being able to see very well. A bald eagle's eyesight is much sharper than a human's.

15

In the Wild

Bald eagles are raptors, or birds of prey. That means they are meat-eating hunters. Bald eagles' favorite food is fish. They can spot a fish in the water from far above. The birds dive down and use sharp talons, or claws, to grab the prey. Bald eagles also hunt rabbits, squirrels, and smaller birds.

Bald eagles are scavengers, too. Scavengers will eat dead animals found in the wild.

Protecting Bald Eagles

In the 1900s, bald eagles were hurt by pesticides, which are poisons used to protect farm crops from harmful insects. Some pesticides also hurt birds and other animals.

People took steps to protect the bald eagle. In 1940, the Eagle Protection Act was passed. The law banned the killing or selling of bald eagles. In 1967, the bald eagle was placed on the Endangered Species List. Special laws were put in place to protect animals on the list.

In 1972, a pesticide called DDT was banned in the United States. After that, the number of bald eagles grew.

Coming Back

Since the 1970s, the bald eagle's numbers have grown. By 1995, it was no longer on the Endangered Species List. However, the bald eagle still needs protection.

Today, growing numbers of bald eagles are born in the wild. Some zoos and wildlife centers breed these special birds, too. With care, America's national emblem will be here to stay.

Bald eagles live for about 30 years in the wild. They often live even longer in zoos and wildlife centers.

Spread the Word

I enjoyed telling you about the bald eagle. Now it's time to get back to work. Our wildlife center protects bald eagles. You, too, can help protect these wonderful birds. Learn as much as you can about bald eagles. Tell your family and friends about them. The bald eagle has a special place in the history of the United States. Everyone should make sure the bird has a place in the future.

Bald Eagle Facts

 The word *bald* usually means "having no hair." It comes from an old word meaning "white." Adult bald eagles have short white feathers on their heads.

 Young bald eagles have brown feathers on their heads.

When diving down to get a fish, a bald eagle can reach speeds of about 100 miles (160 kilometers) per hour.

Bald eagles can swim. When they do, the birds look like they are doing the butterfly stroke.

The largest bald eagle nest on record was 9 feet (2.7 m) across. It weighed more than 2 tons (1.8 metric tons)!

Glossary

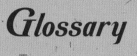

breed — to raise animals or plants

document — an important paper

emblem — a sign or object that stands for something else

Endangered Species List — a U.S. government list of animals in danger of dying out

habitat — the area where an animal lives

prey — an animal hunted as food

raptor — a bird that kills other animals for food

Revolutionary War (1775–1783) — the American Colonies' fight for freedom from Great Britain; the Colonies later became the United States of America

symbol — an object that stands for something else

talons — the sharp claws of an eagle or other bird of prey

wildlife — wild animals living in their natural habitat

To Learn More

At the Library

DeGezelle, Terri. *The Great Seal of the United States*. Mankato, Minn.: Capstone Press, 2004.

Dell, Pamela. *The Bald Eagle*. Minneapolis: Compass Point Books, 2004.

Hempstead, Anne. *The Bald Eagle*. Chicago: Heinemann Library, 2006.

Yanuck, Debbie. *The Bald Eagle*. Mankato, Minn.: Capstone Press, 2003.

On the Web

FactHound offers a safe, fun way to find Web sites related to this book. All of the sites on FactHound have been researched by our staff.

1. Visit *www.facthound.com*

2. Type in this special code: 1404826424

3. Click on the FETCH IT button.

Your trusty FactHound will fetch the best sites for you!

Index

Look for all of the books in the American Symbols series:

The Bald Eagle
The Bill of Rights
The Great Seal of the United States
The Liberty Bell
Our American Flag
Our National Anthem
The Pledge of Allegiance
The Statue of Liberty
The U.S. Constitution
The White House